Remember these 32 teams? 32 TEAMS

The strokes in these Chinese Alphabets are written in this order: ① ② ③ ④ ⑤ ⑥

Q1. Parallel

Q2. Dots (Left to Right)

Q3. Dots (Top to Bottom)

Q4. Final Dot
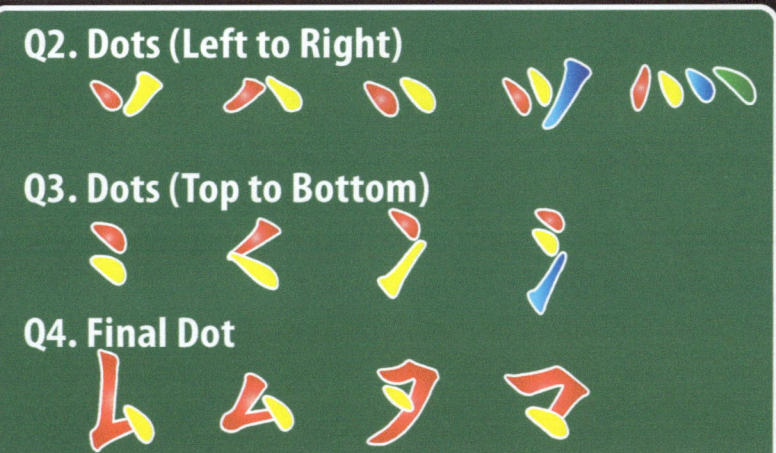

Q5. Half Ladder

Q6. T-Shape

Q7. Split

Q8. Vertical Split
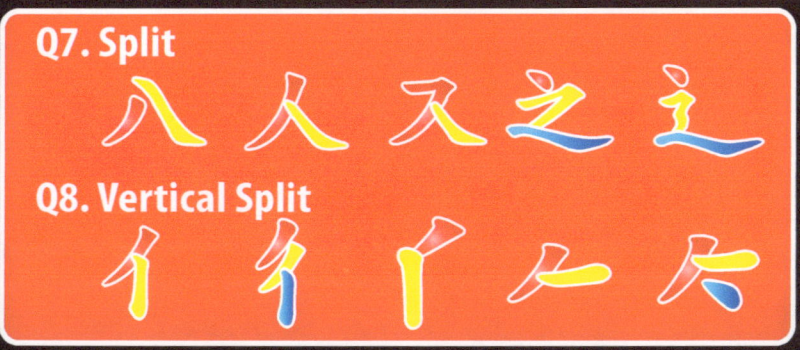

Q9. Slide

Q10. Cross

Q11. 7-Slash

Q12. 7L-Hook
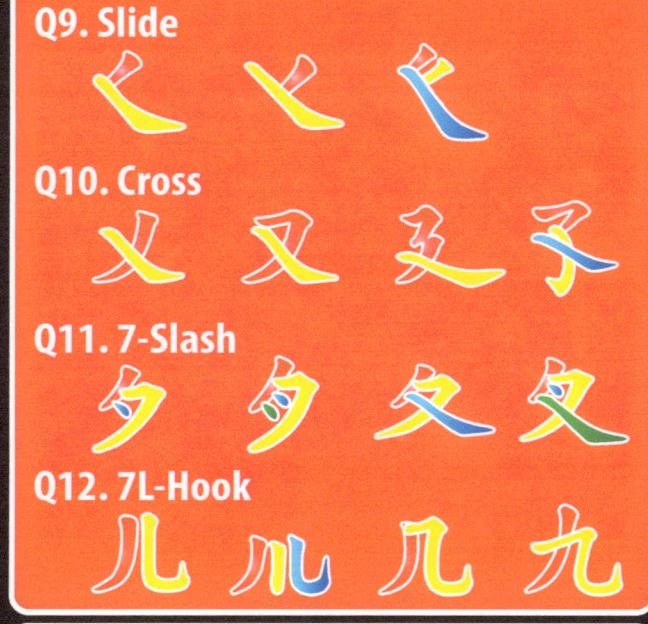

Q13. Marching

Q14. Tick
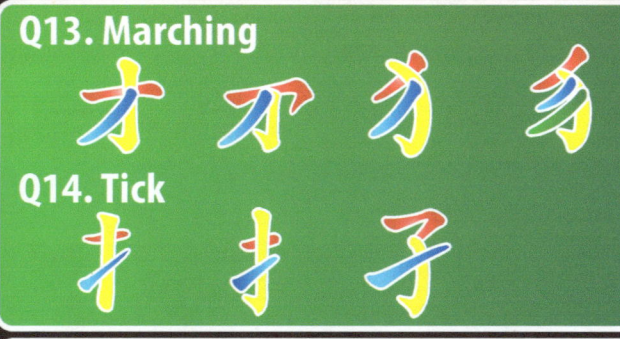

Q15. 7-Hook Flag

Q16. L-Bend Flag
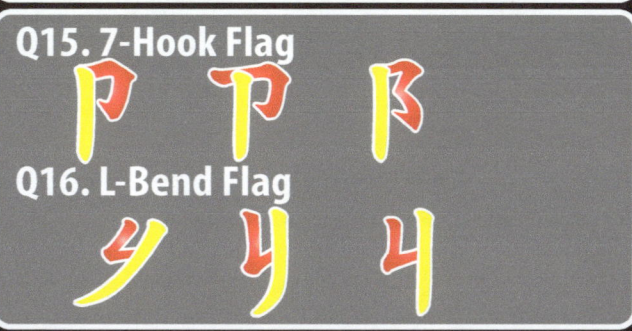

# of CHINESE ALPHABETS

Q17. 7-Hook Frame
刀 力 刀 习

Q18. L-Frame & U-Frame
匕 七 凵 山

Q19. C-Frame
匸 匚 匚 匸 区 巨 臣

Q20. Flipped-C
コ ヨ 彐 卫 凸

Q21. L7-Hook Frame
勹 丂 与 马 乌

Q22. L7-Enclosure
口 夕 马 勻

Q23. n-Frame
冂 刀 门 口

Q24. Skewer
牛 丩 巾 中

Q25. Single Leg
十 千 丫 半 丰 丰

Q26. Multiple Legs
廾 卅 丗 开 井

Q27. Split Intersections
大 天 夫 天 夬

Q28. Tripod
木 未 末 来

Q29. Flat Intersections
土 王 主 玉 丷 並

Q30. Horizontal Enclosure
月 且 目 且 且

Q31. Vertical Enclosure
皿 四 凹 皿

Q32. Intersections Enclosure
田 由 用 冊 曲 曲

1 Parallels Variations

Basic Alphabets

Remove one stroke

 Remove one stroke

Remove one stroke

Change one stroke

Change one stroke

Remove one stroke

二
two

价钱
price

蓝
blue

剑
sword

狮子
lion

汤
soup

2 Final Dot Variations

Basic Alphabets

 Change one stroke ➡ 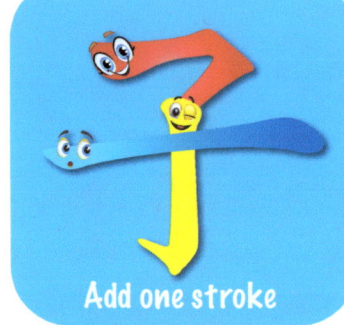 Add one stroke  Change one stroke

辽阔 — vast

行李 — luggage

转 — turn

3 Half Ladder Variations

Basic Alphabets 卜 ㅋ ㅏ ㅌ ㅌ

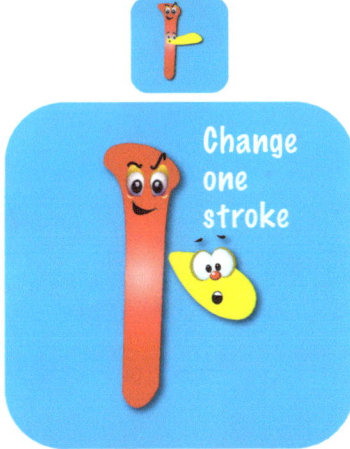
Change one stroke

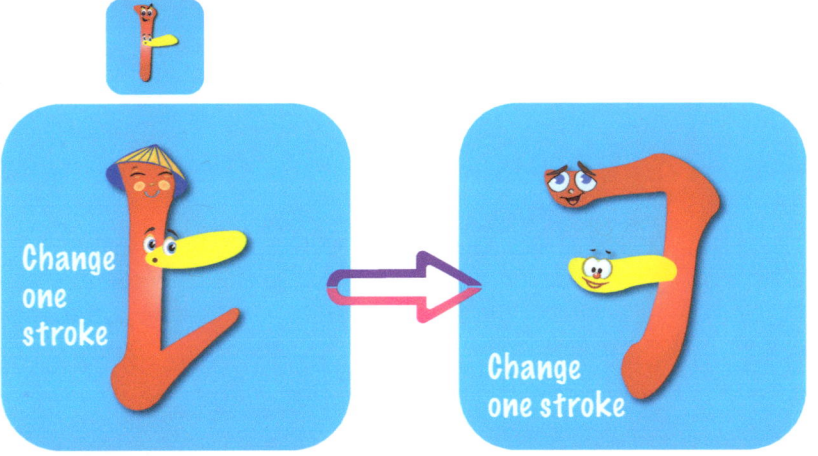
Change one stroke → Change one stroke

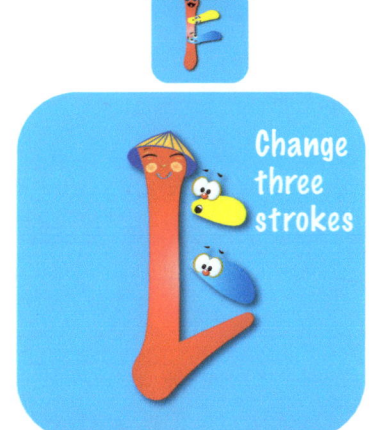
Change three strokes

下
down

毕业帽
graduation cap

陷阱
trap

鼠
rat

4A T-Shape Variations

Basic Alphabets: ㄒ ㄒ ㄒ ㄒ ㄒ ㄒ

 不
Change one stroke

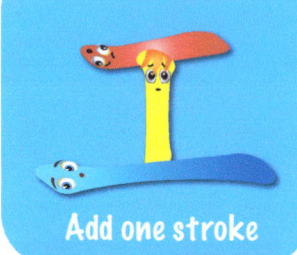 工
Add one stroke

 ㄈ
Change one stroke

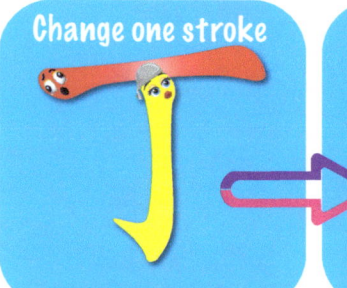 丁
Change one stroke

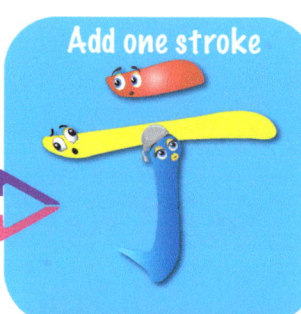 亍
Add one stroke

 丁
Change one stroke

| 石 stone | 工人 worker | 唇 lips | 灯 lamp | 街 street | 野兽 wild animals |

4B T-Shape Variations

Basic Alphabets: L L T T F T

Change one stroke

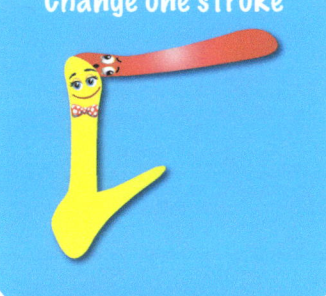

Change one stroke

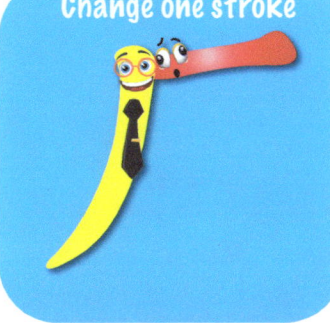

⇒

Change one stroke

跳越
to jump across

铲子
shovel

皮包
leather bag

4C T-Shape Variations

Basic Alphabets: ㅗ ㄴ ㅜ ㅠ ㅜ ㅠ

 **Change one stroke**

 **Change one stroke**
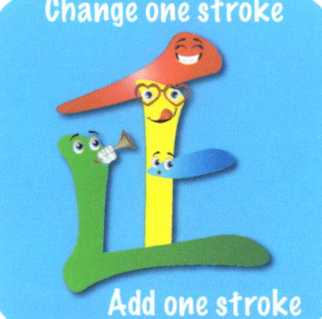
Add one stroke

 **Change one stroke** → **Change one stroke** → **Change one stroke**
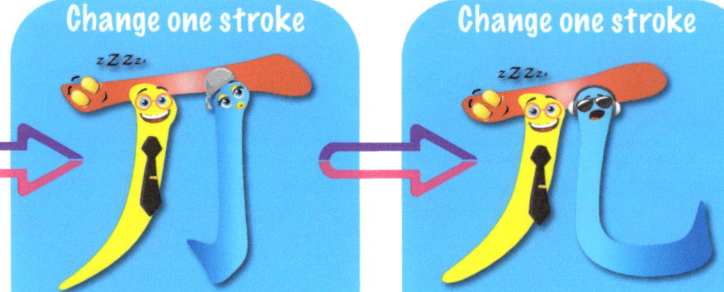

蛋
egg

圣诞
Christmas

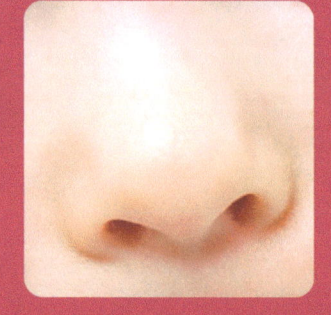
鼻子
nose

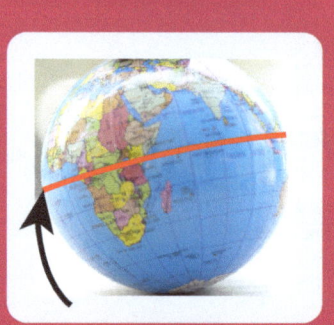
赤道
equator

玩具
toys

5A Vertical Split Variations

Basic Alphabets

亻 亻 亻 一 大

Change one stroke	Change one stroke	Change one stroke	Change one stroke	Add one stroke

农夫
farmer

盾
shield

纸
paper

脚印
footprint

榴莲
durian

5B Vertical Split Variations

Basic Alphabets

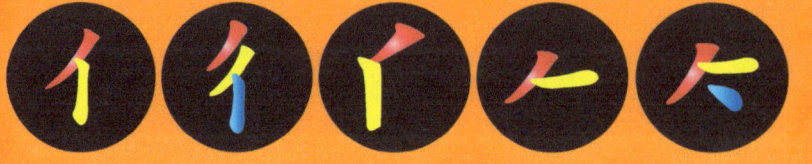

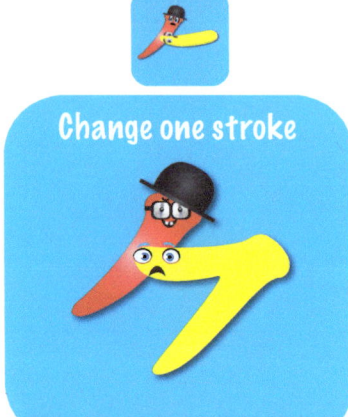 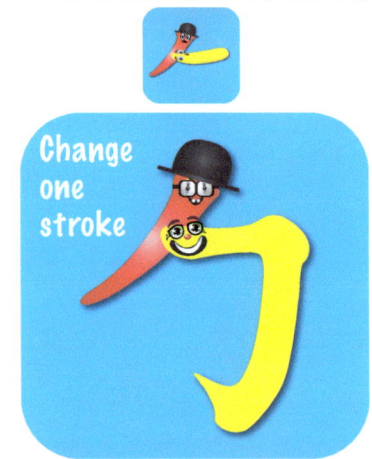 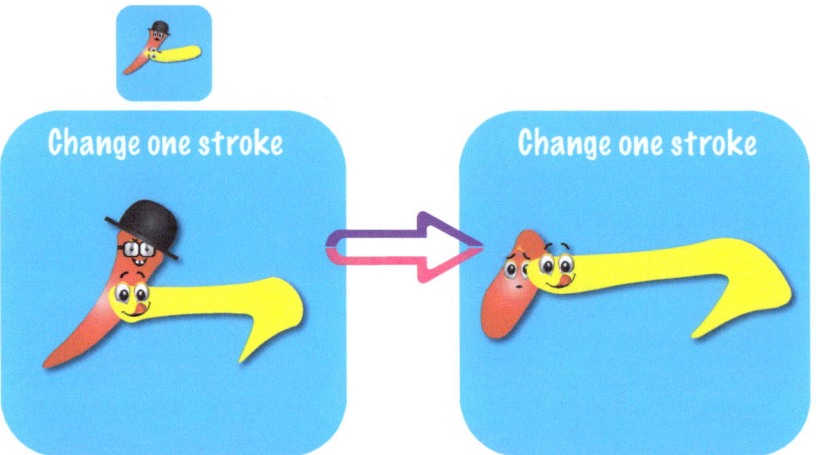

Change one stroke

龟
tortoise

勺子
ladle

吹气球
to blow balloons

窗口
window

6 乙-Hook Variations

Basic Alphabets: 儿 几 几 九

Change one stroke
儿

Shorten one stroke / Strokes become closer
儿

Change one stroke
几

Change one stroke
凡

四
four

兔子
rabbit

船
ship

风
wind

7 Split Variation

Basic Alphabets: 八 人 入 之 之

 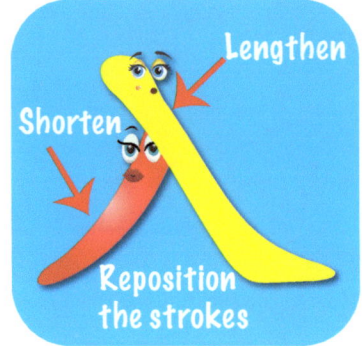  

- Lengthen
- Shorten
- Reposition the strokes

进入 — to enter

8 Slide Variation

Basic Alphabets

Change one stroke

擦 — to wipe

9 — ㄗ-Hook Flag Variations

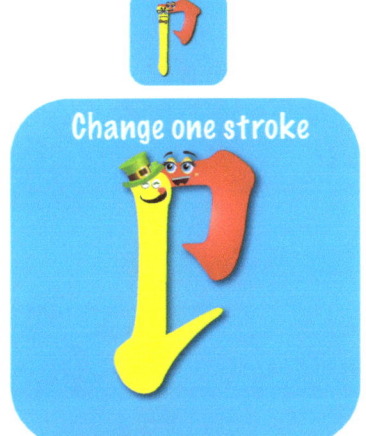
Change one stroke

Change one stroke

10 — L-Bend Flag Variations

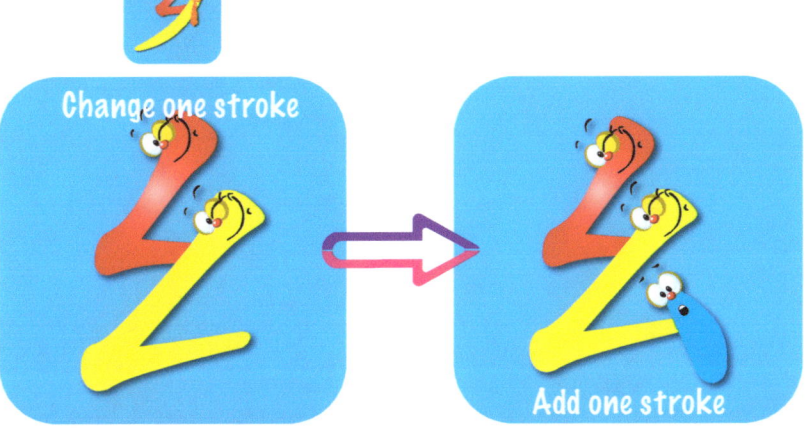
Change one stroke → Add one stroke

顾客
customer

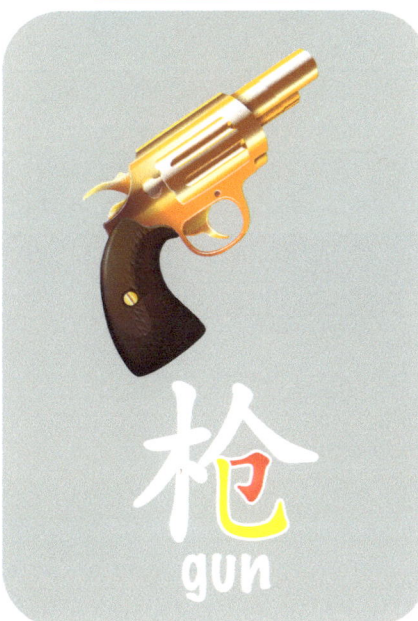
枪
gun

红
red

琴弦
guitar string

Change one stroke

奶
milk

Add one stroke

鸟
bird

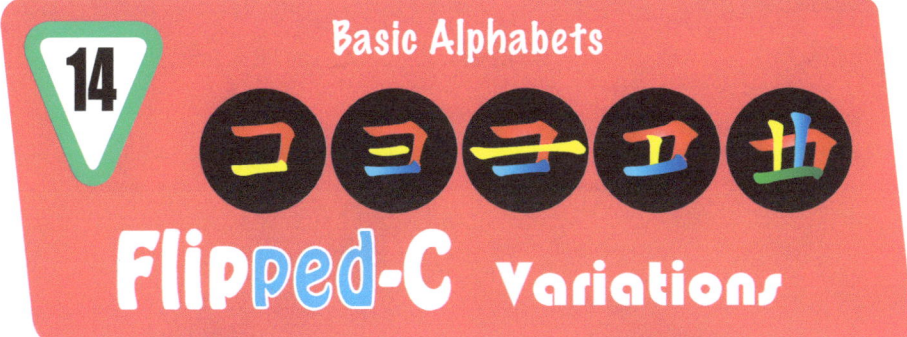

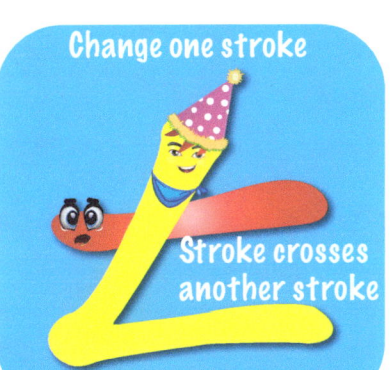

car 车

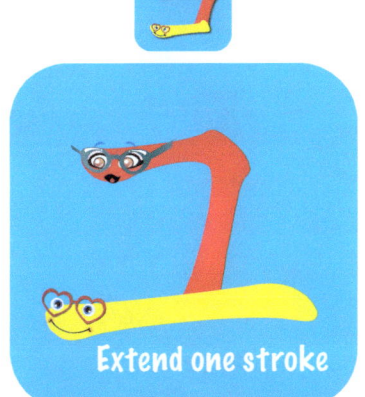

monkey 猴

green 绿色

15A Single Leg Variations — Basic Alphabets

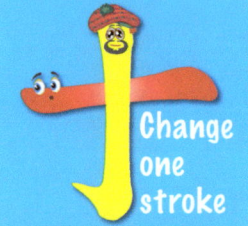 Change one stroke
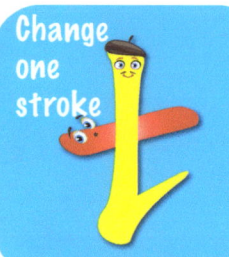 Change one stroke
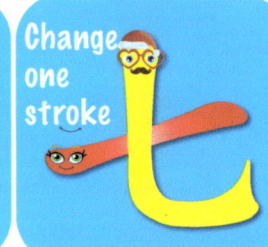 Change one stroke
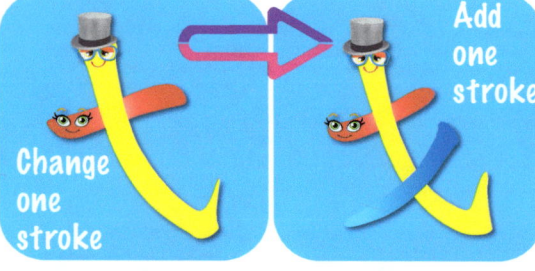 Change one stroke / Add one stroke
 Change one stroke
 Change one stroke

茶 — tea

切片 — to slice

七 — seven

袋鼠 — kangaroo

划船 — to row

朋友 — friends

头发 — hair

15B Single Leg Variations — Basic Alphabets

十 千 ᵶ 千 丰 丰

Change one stroke	Change one stroke	Change one stroke	Extend one stroke	Extend one stroke
干	壬	禾 → 千	千 (Shorten one stroke)	千 (Shorten one stroke)

    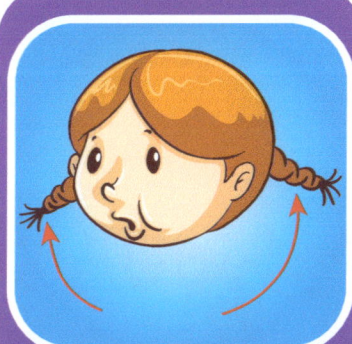

| 芋头 | 锅 | 取暖 | 辣椒 | 辫子 |
| yam | pot | to warm (by a fire) | chilli | braid |

15C Single Leg Variations

Basic Alphabets: 十 干 丰 丰 丰 丰

Change one stroke	Change one stroke	Change one stroke	Change one stroke	Change two strokes
 手	 卡	 才	 毛	 书

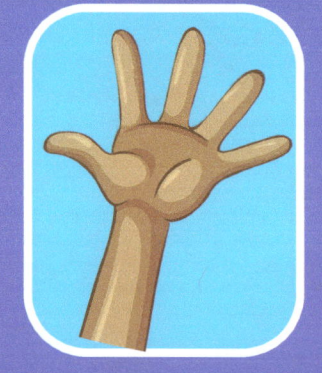

手
hand

撬开
to pry open

看书
to read (a book)

毛笔
brush

书
book

15D Single Leg Variations

Basic Alphabets

Change one stroke

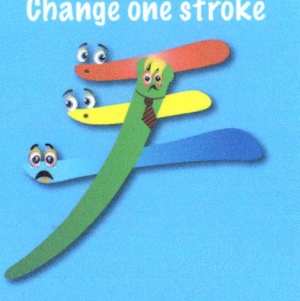

羚羊
antelope

Change one stroke

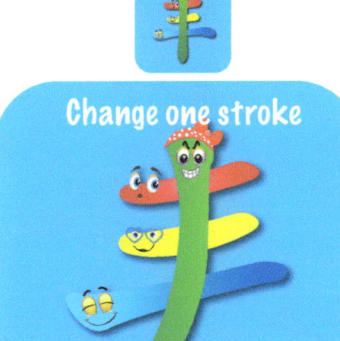

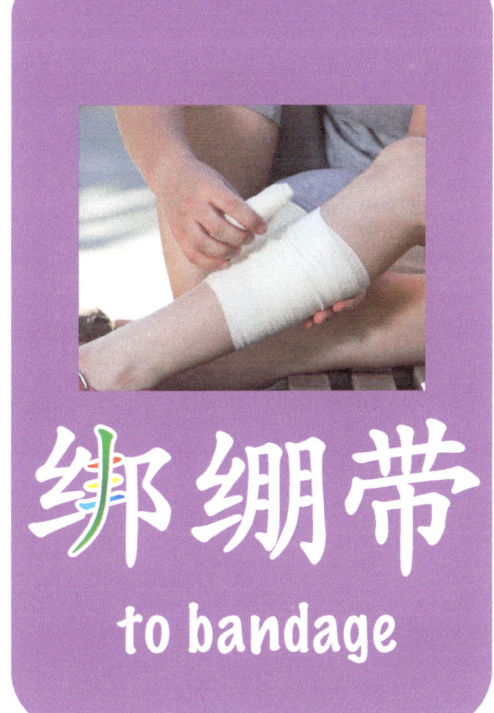

绑绷带
to bandage

Change one stroke

围巾
scarf

16 Flat Intersections Variations

Basic Alphabets

 Extend one stroke / Shorten one stroke

 Extend one stroke / Shorten one stroke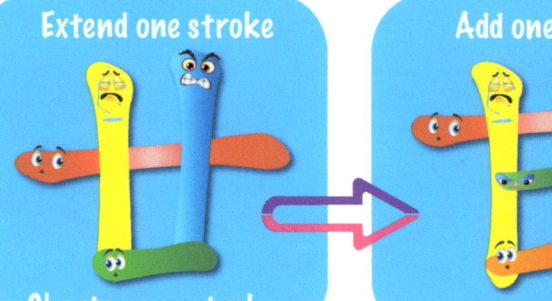

Add one stroke

Add two strokes

No protrusion / Extend one stroke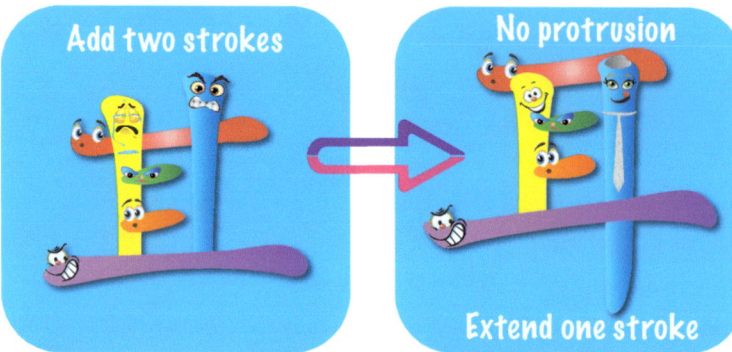

武士 warrior

燕 swallow

甜点 desserts

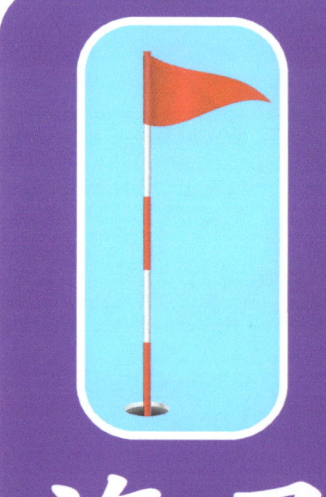
旗子 flag

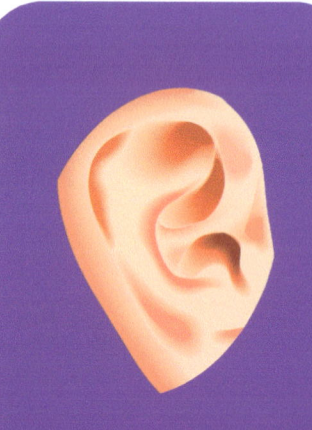
耳朵 ear

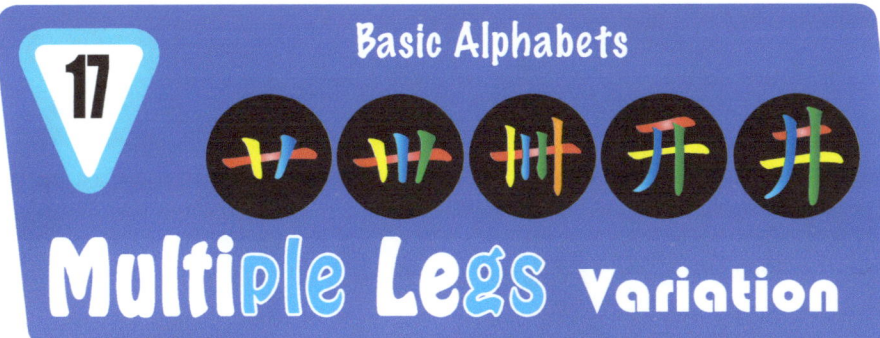

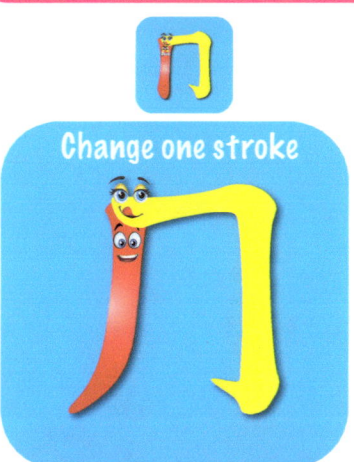

计算器
calculator

独木舟
canoe

英国
England

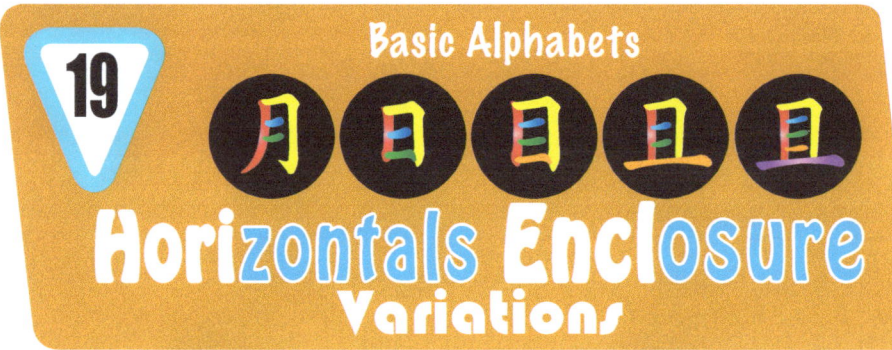

Basic Alphabets
Horizontals Enclosure
Variations

Change one stroke

月 → 冃

Change one stroke / Shorten one stroke

且 → 月

削皮 — to peel (skin)

身体 — body

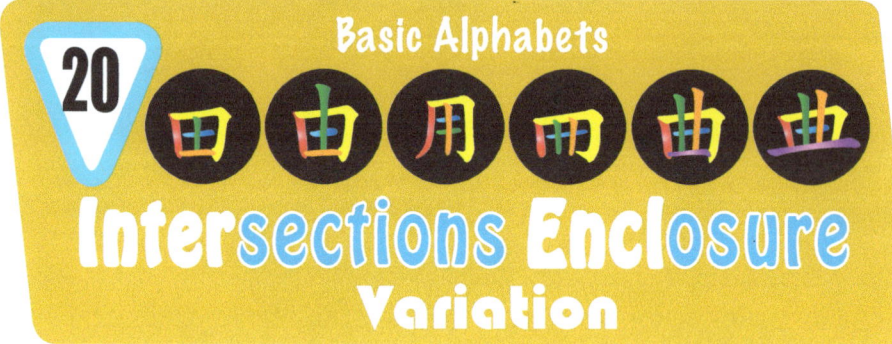

Basic Alphabets
Intersections Enclosure
Variation

Change one stroke

用 → 用

桶 — bucket

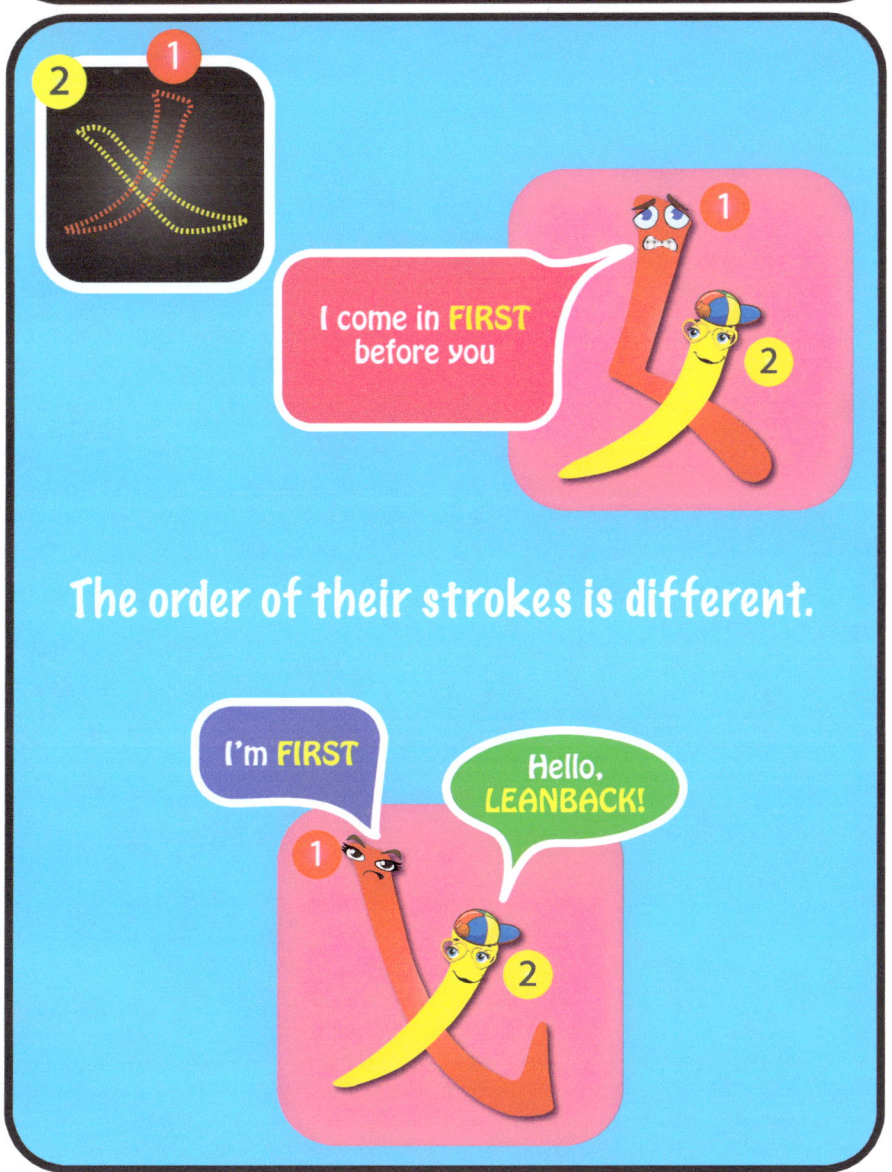

E2 Multiple Legs

Exception

Basic Alphabets

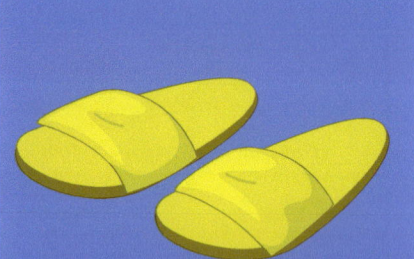

拖鞋
slippers

www.ingramcontent.com/pod-product-compliance
Lightning Source LLC
Chambersburg PA
CBHW050848010526
44107CB00017BA/1221